Title: "Money Queens: Reigning Supreme in Millennial Finance" by Emily S. Miller, International Bestselling Author

Join bestselling author Emily S. Miller on an empowering journey towards financial independence tailored specifically for millennial women. In "Money Queens," Miller presents a comprehensive guide packed with practical advice, relatable anecdotes, and actionable strategies to help women take control of their finances with confidence and flair. From budgeting basics to investment insights and retirement planning, this book equips readers with the tools they need to build wealth, overcome financial challenges, and live life on their own terms. Whether you're just starting your financial journey or looking to level up your money game, "Money Queens" will inspire and empower you to reign supreme in your financial future. Get ready to claim your throne and rule your finances like the queen you are!

Foreword : Welcome to Financial Fabulosity!

Meet Emily: Your Fabulous Financial Guide In this empowering foreword, Emily S. Miller warmly welcomes readers to "Money Queens," where the journey to financial empowerment begins. With her as your guide, get ready to embark on a transformative adventure towards financial freedom.

Chapter 1: Introduction

Meet Emily: Your Fabulous Financial Guide

In this introductory chapter, readers will have the pleasure of meeting Emily S. Miller, your fabulous financial guide through the pages of "Money Queens." Emily introduces herself, sharing her journey to financial independence and her passion for empowering millennial women to take control of their finances. She discusses why financial independence is particularly crucial for women in the millennial generation and sets the stage for what readers can expect from the rest of the book.

Why Financial Independence Matters for Millennial Women

Emily dives into the unique financial challenges faced by millennial women and why achieving financial independence is essential in today's world. From closing the gender pay gap to navigating career interruptions and caregiving responsibilities, Emily highlights the importance of financial empowerment for women of this generation. Through real-life examples and relatable anecdotes, readers will gain insight into the significance of taking charge of their financial futures.

What to Expect from "Money Queens"

In this section, Emily outlines what readers can anticipate from "Money Queens." She sets the tone for the rest of the book, promising a comprehensive guide packed with practical advice, actionable strategies, and empowering insights tailored specifically for millennial women. From mastering budgeting basics to navigating investment options and planning for retirement, Emily assures readers that "Money Queens" will equip them with the tools they need to reign supreme in their financial lives.

Chapter 2: Money Mindset Makeover

Breaking Free from Financial Fears and Limiting Beliefs

In this chapter, Emily helps readers identify and overcome common financial fears and limiting beliefs that may be holding them back from achieving their financial goals. She provides practical strategies for reframing negative thoughts about money and cultivating a positive mindset that fosters financial growth and empowerment. Through personal anecdotes and actionable tips, Emily empowers readers to confront their fears head-on and embrace a mindset of abundance and possibility.

Cultivating a Wealth Mindset: You Are Your Greatest Asset

Emily emphasizes the importance of cultivating a wealth mindset and recognizing oneself as the greatest asset in the pursuit of financial independence. She explores the concept of self-worth and its connection to financial success, encouraging readers to invest in their personal and professional development. Through mindset-shifting exercises and empowering affirmations, Emily guides readers on a journey of self-discovery and self-empowerment, laying the foundation for building wealth and abundance in all areas of life.

Embracing the Journey to Financial Independence with Confidence

In this final section of Chapter 2, Emily inspires readers to embrace the journey to financial independence with confidence and determination. She shares her own experiences and challenges on the path to financial freedom, offering encouragement and support to readers facing similar obstacles. Through practical strategies for overcoming setbacks and staying focused on long-term goals, Emily empowers readers to take ownership of their financial futures and embark on a journey of self-discovery, growth, and financial empowerment.

Chapter 3: Building a Solid Financial Foundation

Understanding Your Current Financial Situation

Emily kicks off this chapter by guiding readers through the process of understanding their current financial situation. She provides practical tools and exercises to help readers assess their income, expenses, assets, and liabilities. By gaining clarity on their financial standing, readers can identify areas for improvement and set realistic goals for financial growth. Emily emphasizes the importance of honesty and self-awareness in this process, laying the groundwork for building a strong financial foundation.

Budgeting Basics Made Easy

In this section, Emily demystifies budgeting and makes it approachable for readers of all financial backgrounds. She introduces simple yet effective budgeting techniques and tools to help readers take control of their spending and prioritize their financial goals. From creating a monthly budget to tracking expenses and adjusting spending habits, Emily provides practical tips and real-life examples to empower readers to create a budget that works for them. By mastering budgeting basics, readers can gain confidence in managing their finances and lay the groundwork for long-term financial success.

The Power of Emergency Funds: Your Financial Safety Net

Emily highlights the importance of building an emergency fund as a critical component of financial security. She explains what an emergency fund is, why it's essential, and how to start saving for one. Emily provides practical advice on setting savings goals, automating contributions, and finding creative ways to boost emergency fund savings. By emphasizing the peace of mind and financial stability that an emergency fund provides, Emily empowers readers to prioritize saving and take control of their financial futures.

Chapter 4: Decoding Investments: From Stocks to Real Estate

Investing 101: Demystifying Stocks, Bonds, and Mutual Funds

In this chapter, Emily simplifies the world of investing by breaking down key concepts and investment options. She introduces readers to stocks, bonds, and mutual funds, explaining how each works and their potential benefits and risks. Emily provides guidance on how to start investing, including choosing the right investment account and setting investment goals. Through relatable examples and clear explanations, Emily empowers readers to overcome their fear of investing and take the first steps towards building wealth through investment.

Exploring Alternative Investments: Real Estate, Cryptocurrency, and Beyond

In this section, Emily expands readers' investment horizons by exploring alternative investment opportunities beyond traditional stocks and bonds. She introduces real estate investment, cryptocurrency, and other alternative assets, explaining their potential benefits and risks. Emily provides practical advice on how to evaluate alternative investment options, conduct thorough research, and diversify investment portfolios. By showcasing the potential for wealth accumulation through alternative investments, Emily encourages readers to consider new avenues for growing their wealth.

Diversification: The Key to Building a Resilient Investment Portfolio

Emily emphasizes the importance of diversification in building a resilient investment portfolio that can withstand market fluctuations. She explains the concept of diversification and its role in managing investment risk. Emily provides practical strategies for diversifying investment portfolios across asset classes, industries, and geographic regions. Through real-life examples and case studies, Emily illustrates the benefits of diversification and empowers readers to create well-balanced investment portfolios tailored to their financial goals and risk tolerance.

Chapter 5: Retirement Planning for Millennials

Why Retirement Planning Matters, Even in Your 20s

In this chapter, Emily underscores the importance of early retirement planning for millennial women, regardless of their age. She discusses the unique challenges millennials face, such as longer life expectancies and the uncertainty of Social Security, and emphasizes the need to start saving for retirement as early as possible. Emily provides compelling reasons why retirement planning matters, even in one's twenties, and offers practical tips for getting started on the path to financial security in retirement.

Navigating Employer-Sponsored Retirement Accounts: 401(k), 403(b), and IRA

Emily guides readers through the landscape of employer-sponsored retirement accounts, including 401(k), 403(b), and Individual Retirement Accounts (IRA). She explains how these accounts work, the tax advantages they offer, and how to maximize their benefits. Emily provides clear and actionable advice on how to choose the right retirement account, navigate investment options, and optimize contributions to achieve long-term financial goals. By demystifying employer-sponsored retirement accounts, Emily empowers readers to take full advantage of these valuable retirement savings tools.

The Magic of Compound Interest: Starting Early for a Wealthy Retirement

In this section, Emily unveils the power of compound interest and its profound impact on building wealth for retirement. She explains how compound interest works and demonstrates the significant advantage of starting to save for retirement early. Emily provides practical examples and illustrations to help readers understand the exponential growth potential of their retirement savings over time. By harnessing the magic of compound interest, Emily inspires readers to take action and prioritize retirement savings to secure a financially abundant future.

Chapter 6: Building Wealth at Any Age

Investing Strategies for Every Stage of Life: 20s, 30s, 40s, and Beyond

In this chapter, Emily presents tailored investment strategies for women at different stages of life, from their twenties to retirement age and beyond. She highlights the importance of aligning investment strategies with individual financial goals, risk tolerance, and life circumstances. Emily provides practical guidance on asset allocation, portfolio diversification, and investment vehicle selection based on age and financial objectives. By offering personalized investment advice for each life stage, Emily empowers readers to make informed decisions and build wealth steadily throughout their lives.

Overcoming Common Financial Challenges: Debt, Student Loans, and More

Emily addresses common financial challenges faced by millennial women, including debt, student loans, and other financial obligations. She offers practical strategies for managing and reducing debt, such as budgeting, debt consolidation, and student loan repayment options. Emily provides empathetic support and guidance to help readers navigate financial setbacks and regain control of their financial futures. By offering actionable solutions and encouragement, Emily empowers readers to overcome financial obstacles and move forward on the path to financial freedom.

Turning Financial Goals into Actionable Plans: Dream Big, Achieve Bigger

Synopsis: In this final section of Chapter 6, Emily encourages readers to turn their financial goals into actionable plans for success. She emphasizes the importance of setting specific, measurable, achievable, relevant, and time-bound (SMART) goals and outlines a step-by-step process for creating a financial action plan. Emily provides practical tips for goal setting, prioritizing financial objectives, and tracking progress over time. By empowering readers to dream big and take decisive action, Emily inspires them to achieve their financial aspirations and build a future of abundance and fulfillment.

Chapter 7: Protecting Your Financial Future

Understanding Insurance Basics: Health, Life, and Disability

Synopsis: In this chapter, Emily delves into the fundamentals of insurance and its critical role in protecting one's financial future. She explains the importance of health insurance for safeguarding against unexpected medical expenses and provides guidance on choosing the right coverage. Emily also discusses the significance of life insurance in providing financial security for loved ones and explores disability insurance as a vital safeguard against income loss due to disability. By demystifying insurance basics, Emily empowers readers to make informed decisions to protect themselves and their families from financial risks.

Estate Planning Made Simple: Wills, Trusts, and Power of Attorney

Emily guides readers through the essential components of estate planning, including wills, trusts, and powers of attorney. She explains the importance of estate planning in ensuring one's assets are distributed according to their wishes and provides practical advice on creating a comprehensive estate plan. Emily also discusses the role of trusts in asset protection and the importance of appointing a power of attorney for financial and healthcare decisions. By simplifying estate planning concepts, Emily empowers readers to take proactive steps to protect their estates and legacy for future generations.

Safeguarding Your Wealth: Strategies to Protect Against Financial Risks

In this final section of Chapter 7, Emily explores additional strategies for safeguarding wealth and mitigating financial risks. She discusses the importance of asset protection through strategies such as liability insurance, umbrella policies, and legal entities like LLCs and trusts. Emily also addresses cybersecurity risks and provides tips for protecting personal and financial information from online threats. By equipping readers with practical risk management strategies, Emily empowers them to preserve their hard-earned wealth and achieve greater peace of mind in their financial lives.

Chapter 8: Navigating Financial Milestones with Grace

Buying Your First Home: Tips for Millennial Homebuyers

In this chapter, Emily provides valuable insights and practical tips for millennial women navigating the process of buying their first home. She discusses key considerations such as budgeting for a down payment, understanding mortgage options, and navigating the homebuying process. Emily also offers advice on finding the right real estate agent, evaluating neighborhoods, and negotiating purchase offers. By demystifying the homebuying process and offering guidance every step of the way, Emily empowers millennial women to achieve their dream of homeownership with confidence and grace.

Planning for Marriage and Family: Combining Finances with Your Partner

Emily explores the complexities of combining finances with a partner and planning for marriage and family. She discusses the importance of open communication, shared financial goals, and mutual respect in building a strong financial foundation as a couple. Emily offers practical advice on merging finances, creating joint budgets, and navigating financial decisions together. She also addresses the importance of financial compatibility and the role of prenuptial agreements in protecting individual assets. By empowering couples to approach financial planning as a team, Emily helps them lay the groundwork for a successful and harmonious financial future together.

Achieving Financial Independence: Your Ticket to Freedom and Fulfillment

In this final section of Chapter 8, Emily explores the concept of financial independence and its profound impact on one's quality of life. She defines financial independence as the ability to live comfortably and pursue one's passions without being reliant on a traditional job or paycheck. Emily discusses the principles of FIRE (Financial Independence, Retire Early) and offers practical strategies for achieving financial independence at any age. By inspiring readers to envision a life of freedom and fulfillment, Emily empowers them to take proactive steps towards financial independence and design the life of their dreams.

Chapter 9: Cultivating Financial Confidence and Empowerment

Celebrating Your Financial Wins: Small Victories Lead to Big Successes

In this chapter, Emily encourages readers to celebrate their financial wins, no matter how small. She emphasizes the importance of recognizing and acknowledging progress on the financial journey, whether it's paying off debt, reaching a savings goal, or making a successful investment. Emily shares strategies for celebrating financial victories, such as rewarding oneself, sharing achievements with loved ones, and reflecting on personal growth. By celebrating every step forward, Emily empowers readers to build confidence and momentum on their path to financial success.

Embracing Financial Challenges: Turning Setbacks into Comebacks

Emily addresses the inevitable financial challenges and setbacks that readers may encounter along their journey. She reframes setbacks as opportunities for growth and resilience, offering practical strategies for overcoming obstacles and bouncing back stronger than ever. Emily shares personal anecdotes of overcoming financial challenges and provides encouragement and support to readers facing similar struggles. By embracing challenges as learning experiences and opportunities for growth, Emily empowers readers to persevere in the face of adversity and continue moving forward on their financial journey.

Paying It Forward: Empowering Other Women on Their Financial Journeys

In this final section of Chapter 9, Emily inspires readers to pay it forward by empowering other women on their financial journeys. She discusses the importance of community and collaboration in achieving financial goals and encourages readers to share their knowledge, experiences, and resources with others. Emily provides suggestions for ways to support and uplift fellow women, such as mentorship, financial education initiatives, and advocacy for gender equality in finance. By fostering a culture of support and empowerment, Emily empowers readers to make a positive impact on the lives of others and create a more inclusive and equitable financial future for all.

Chapter 10: Conclusion

Your Fabulous Financial Future Starts Now: Take Action, Live Your Dreams

Synopsis: In this concluding chapter, Emily reinforces the message that financial empowerment is achievable for every millennial woman. She urges readers to take the knowledge and insights gained from "Money Queens" and apply them to their own lives with determination and enthusiasm. Emily emphasizes the importance of setting concrete financial goals, staying committed to personal growth, and embracing the journey with optimism and resilience. By empowering readers to take control of their financial destinies, Emily inspires them to step into their power and pursue their dreams with confidence and purpose.

Stay Inspired: Resources for Your Financial Journey

In this final section of Chapter 10, Emily provides readers with a curated list of resources to support them on their financial journey. She suggests books, podcasts, websites, and online communities where readers can find additional guidance, inspiration, and support. Emily encourages readers to explore these resources, connect with other like-minded individuals, and continue their financial education and empowerment beyond the pages of "Money Queens." By providing a roadmap for ongoing learning and growth, Emily ensures that readers have the tools and support they need to thrive on their journey to financial independence.

Foreword

Welcome to "Money Queens," where your journey to financial empowerment begins. As the author of this book, Emily S. Miller, I am thrilled to be your guide on this transformative adventure.

I remember vividly the moment when I realized the power of financial independence. It wasn't just about having a hefty bank account or fancy possessions—it was about freedom, autonomy, and the ability to live life on my own terms. My journey to financial freedom was not without its challenges. I faced setbacks, made mistakes, and encountered obstacles along the way. But through perseverance, determination, and a deep-seated belief in myself, I overcame those challenges and emerged stronger and more resilient than ever.

As a millennial woman navigating the complexities of the modern world, I understand firsthand the unique challenges and opportunities we face. From juggling student loans and entry-level salaries to navigating career transitions and planning for the future, I've been there. And I'm here to tell you that financial independence is not just a dream reserved for the lucky few—it's an achievable goal for each and every one of us.

In "Money Queens," I share the insights, strategies, and lessons learned from my own journey to financial freedom. From budgeting basics to investment strategies, retirement planning to wealth building, this book is your comprehensive guide to mastering your finances and reclaiming your power.

But more than just practical advice, "Money Queens" is a celebration of sisterhood, empowerment, and the limitless potential of women. It's about supporting each other, lifting each other up, and cheering each other on as we chart our own paths to success.

So, dear reader, I invite you to join me on this empowering journey. Together, we'll navigate the twists and turns of the financial landscape, celebrate your successes, and overcome any obstacles that come our way. Because when women support each other, incredible things happen.

Get ready to reign supreme as the queen of your finances. Your fabulous financial future starts now.

With love and empowerment,

Emily Miller

Emily S. Miller

Chapter 1.1: Meet Emily: Your Fabulous Financial Guide

Hey there, fabulous readers! I'm Emily S. Miller, your go-to gal for all things money-related in "Money Queens." Buckle up, because we're about to embark on a journey that will change the way you think about finances forever.

Now, let me start by telling you a bit about myself. I wasn't always the money-savvy queen you see before you. Nope, I've had my fair share of financial fumbles and slip-ups along the way. From maxing out credit cards to living paycheck to paycheck, I've been through it all. But you know what? Those challenges only made me stronger and more determined to take control of my financial future.

That's right, I'm a proud millennial woman, just like you. And let me tell you, I get it. I understand the struggles we face in today's world—the student loan debt, the sky-high rent, the pressure to keep up with the Joneses. But here's the thing: I refuse to let those challenges hold me back, and I refuse to let them hold you back either.

That's why I'm so passionate about empowering millennial women like you to take charge of your finances and live life on your own terms. Because let's face it, financial independence isn't just about having a fat bank account (although that's certainly nice). It's about freedom, autonomy, and the ability to pursue your passions without being shackled to a 9-to-5 grind.

In "Money Queens," I'll be sharing all the tips, tricks, and strategies I've learned along my own journey to financial freedom. From budgeting hacks to investment secrets, retirement planning to wealth building, consider me your personal financial fairy godmother, here to sprinkle a little magic dust on your money matters.

But more than just practical advice, "Money Queens" is a celebration of sisterhood and solidarity. It's about women lifting each other up, supporting each other's dreams, and smashing through glass ceilings together. So get ready to join a community of like-minded queens who are ready to rule their finances and take the world by storm.

Are you excited? Because I sure am. Together, we're going to rewrite the rules of money and create a future that's as fabulous as you are. So grab your crown, darling, and let's reign supreme as the queens of our own financial destinies!

Chapter 1.2: Why Financial Independence Matters for Millennial Women

Alright, let's get real, ladies. We're living in a world where the deck often feels stacked against us, especially when it comes to money. But guess what? We're not going to let that stop us from slaying our financial goals and living our best lives.

As millennial women, we face a unique set of financial challenges that our predecessors may not have encountered. We're still grappling with a persistent gender pay gap that sees us earning less than our male counterparts for the same work. Add to that the fact that many of us are juggling career interruptions—whether it's taking time off to care for children or aging parents—and it's no wonder that achieving financial independence can feel like an uphill battle.

But here's the thing: we refuse to be held back by outdated stereotypes or societal expectations. We're fierce, we're fabulous, and we're ready to take control of our financial futures like the queens we are.

That's why financial independence isn't just a lofty goal for us—it's a non-negotiable necessity. It's about more than just having enough money to pay the bills (although that's certainly important). It's about having the freedom to make choices that align with our values and priorities, whether that means traveling the world, starting our own businesses, or giving back to our communities.

In "Money Queens," I'll be diving deep into the why behind financial independence for millennial women. Through real-life examples and relatable anecdotes, you'll gain insight into the significance of taking charge of your financial future. Because when we empower ourselves with knowledge and action, there's nothing we can't achieve.

So buckle up, my fellow queens, because we're about to embark on a journey that will change the way you think about money—and change your life in the process. Get ready to slay your financial goals and reign supreme as the queens of your own destinies. Let's do this!

Chapter 1.3: What to Expect from "Money Queens"

Alright, ladies, let's talk about what you can expect from this fabulous journey we're about to embark on together. Consider this your sneak peek into the treasure trove of wisdom and empowerment that awaits you within the pages of "Money Queens."

First things first, let me set the tone for what's to come. This isn't your average finance book filled with mind-numbing jargon and complex equations. No way, honey. "Money Queens" is your ultimate guide to financial empowerment, tailored specifically for millennial women like you.

I'm talking about a comprehensive roadmap packed with practical advice, actionable strategies, and empowering insights that will leave you feeling like the queen of your financial castle. From mastering the basics of budgeting to diving deep into investment options and planning for retirement like a boss, we're covering it all.

But here's the best part: I've designed "Money Queens" to be more than just a how-to manual. It's a journey of self-discovery, empowerment, and transformation. Along the way, you'll not only learn how to manage your money like a pro but also uncover your own inner strength and resilience.

So get ready to roll up your sleeves and dive headfirst into the world of personal finance. Whether you're a total newbie or a seasoned pro looking to level up your money game, "Money Queens" has something for everyone. Consider it your secret weapon for conquering your financial fears and reclaiming your power.

By the time you reach the final page, you'll be armed with the tools, knowledge, and confidence you need to reign supreme in your financial life. So buckle up, queens, because we're about to embark on a journey that will change the way you think about money—and change your life in the process. Let's slay!

Chapter 2.1: Money Mindset Makeover

Breaking Free from Financial Fears and Limiting Beliefs

Welcome to Chapter 2 of "Money Queens," where we're diving deep into the heart of our financial mindset. Today, we're going to confront those nagging fears and limiting beliefs that have been holding you back from achieving your full financial potential. Get ready to roll up your sleeves and get to work, because we're about to unleash your inner money queen!

Identifying Your Financial Fears and Limiting Beliefs:

Let's start by shining a spotlight on those fears and beliefs that have been lurking in the shadows of your mind. Take a few moments to grab a pen and paper and jot down any thoughts or beliefs you have about money that may be holding you back. Are you afraid of never being able to get out of debt? Do you believe that you'll never earn enough to live comfortably? Whatever it is, write it down—acknowledging these beliefs is the first step towards overcoming them.

Reframing Negative Thoughts:

Now that you've identified your financial fears and limiting beliefs, it's time to reframe them into more empowering perspectives. Let's take that belief of never being able to get out of debt, for example. Instead of seeing it as a permanent condition, try reframing it as a temporary challenge that you're actively working to overcome. By shifting your mindset from one of defeat to one of resilience and determination, you'll open yourself up to new possibilities and opportunities.

Cultivating a Positive Money Mindset:

Next up, let's focus on cultivating a positive money mindset that fosters growth and empowerment. One powerful technique is the use of affirmations—positive statements that you repeat to yourself regularly to reinforce empowering beliefs about money. For example, you might say "I am worthy of financial abundance" or "Money flows to me effortlessly and abundantly." By consistently affirming these positive beliefs, you'll begin to reprogram your subconscious mind for success.

Visualizing Your Financial Goals:

Visualization is another powerful tool for cultivating a positive money mindset. Take some time each day to vividly imagine yourself achieving your financial goals with clarity and detail. Picture yourself debt-free, financially secure, and living your dream life. What does it look like? How does it feel? By visualizing your desired outcomes with intensity and emotion, you'll create a powerful magnet that draws you closer to your goals.

Taking Action:

Finally, remember that mindset alone isn't enough—you also need to take action towards your financial goals. Break your goals down into smaller, manageable steps, and commit to taking consistent action towards them every day. Whether it's setting up a budget, paying off debt, or investing in your future, every small step you take brings you closer to financial empowerment.

Congratulations, Money Queens, you've completed Chapter 2 of "Money Queens" and taken a giant leap towards transforming your money mindset. Remember, overcoming your financial fears and limiting beliefs is a journey, not a destination. Be patient with yourself, celebrate your progress, and keep moving forward with confidence and determination. Your financial future is bright, and you have everything you need to achieve your wildest dreams.

Chapter 2.2: Cultivating a Wealth Mindset: You Are Your Greatest Asset

Recognizing Your Value: You Are Your Greatest Asset

Welcome back, Money Queens, to Chapter 2 of "Money Queens," where we're diving deep into the transformative power of cultivating a wealth mindset. Today, we're going to explore the concept of self-worth and its profound connection to financial success. Get ready to embark on a journey of self-discovery and self-empowerment, because you, my dear, are your greatest asset!

Understanding Your Value:

Let's start by acknowledging something that's often overlooked in the world of personal finance: you are priceless. Your talents, skills, and unique perspective are invaluable assets that have the power to shape your financial future. But here's the kicker: in order to unlock their full potential, you need to recognize and honor your own worth.

Investing in Yourself:

Now that we've established your value as an individual, it's time to start investing in yourself like the boss queen you are. Prioritize your personal and professional development through further education, skills training, or self-improvement courses. By continually investing in yourself, you enhance your earning potential and lay the foundation for long-term financial success.

Shifting Your Mindset:

Cultivating a wealth mindset means shifting from scarcity to abundance. Let go of limiting beliefs about your worthiness and embrace a mindset of limitless possibility. Repeat after me: "I am worthy of success and abundance in all areas of my life." Believe it, own it, and watch as the universe conspires to make it a reality.

Taking Inspired Action:

Mindset alone isn't enough—you also need to take inspired action. Set clear intentions, make strategic plans, and take consistent steps towards your vision of financial abundance. Whether it's starting a side hustle, networking, or seeking mentorship, every action brings you closer to your dreams.

Recognizing Your Value in Action:

Let's put theory into practice with a powerful exercise. Take a few moments to reflect on your unique strengths, talents, and achievements. Write them down and celebrate them as evidence of your worthiness and potential. Remember, you are your greatest asset, and the world is waiting for you to shine your light brightly.

Remember, by recognizing your value, investing in yourself, and embracing abundance, you're laying the foundation for wealth and success. Keep shining, queens!

Chapter 2.3: Embracing the Journey to Financial Independence with Confidence

Stepping into Your Financial Power: Embrace the Journey with Confidence

Welcome back, Money Queens, to the final section of Chapter 2 in "Money Queens," where we're delving into the heart of the journey to financial independence. Today, we're exploring how you can embrace this journey with unwavering confidence, determination, and a fierce sense of empowerment. Let's dive in and empower ourselves to take charge of our financial futures like the queens we are!

Acknowledging Your Journey:

Let's start by recognizing that the road to financial independence isn't always smooth sailing. It's filled with twists, turns, and unexpected challenges. But every obstacle we encounter is an opportunity for growth and learning. By acknowledging the journey ahead, we empower ourselves to face it head-on with courage and resilience.

Sharing My Journey:

I want to share some of my own experiences and challenges on the path to financial freedom. Like many of you, I've faced setbacks and doubts along the way. But through perseverance and a belief in my own abilities, I've learned to overcome obstacles and stay focused on my goals. Remember, your journey is unique to you, but you're not alone in facing its challenges.

Overcoming Setbacks:

Setbacks are a natural part of any journey, but they don't define us. Whether it's a job loss, unexpected expenses, or a financial misstep, setbacks are opportunities for growth and course-correction. Instead of letting setbacks derail us, let's use them as fuel to propel ourselves forward with even greater determination and resilience.

Staying Focused on Long-Term Goals:

In a world of instant gratification, staying focused on long-term goals can be challenging. But remember, every small step you take today brings you closer to your future financial freedom. Stay disciplined, stay focused, and never lose sight of the bigger picture. Your future self will thank you for the sacrifices you make today.

Taking Ownership of Your Financial Future:

Ultimately, achieving financial independence is about taking ownership of our financial futures. It's about believing in our worth, setting ambitious goals, and taking proactive steps to achieve them. By embracing the journey with confidence and determination, we empower ourselves to create the lives we've always dreamed of.

Remember, setbacks are temporary, but our determination is permanent. Stay focused, stay resilient, and keep moving forward. Your financial freedom awaits, and you have everything you need to achieve it. Keep shining, queens!

Chapter 3.1: Building a Solid Financial Foundation

Laying the Groundwork: Understanding Your Financial Landscape

Welcome, Money Queens, to Chapter 3 of "Money Queens," where we're rolling up our sleeves and getting down to the nitty-gritty of building a rock-solid financial foundation. Today, I'll guide you through the process of understanding your current financial situation—a crucial step on our journey to financial independence. So grab your notebooks and let's get started on laying the groundwork for your financial success!

Assessing Your Financial Landscape:

Let's kick things off by taking a close look at your current financial situation. We need to understand where you stand before we can chart a course for where you want to go. So grab a pen and paper, and let's dive in together!

Understanding Your Income:

First up, let's assess your income sources. This includes your salary, wages, bonuses, freelance earnings, or any other money coming in. It's important to account for all sources of income, no matter how big or small. Understanding your income streams will give us a clear picture of your earning potential and help us craft a solid financial plan.

Tracking Your Expenses:

Next, let's get real about your spending habits. Take a deep dive into your expenses—both fixed and variable. Be honest with yourself about where your money is going each month. Tracking your expenses will help us identify areas where we can cut back and give us insight into your financial priorities and values.

Assessing Your Assets:

Now, let's turn our attention to your assets—the things you own that have value. This could include your savings accounts, investments, retirement accounts, real estate, or any other assets you may have. Knowing your assets will give us a sense of your financial strength and stability and lay the groundwork for building wealth over time.

Understanding Your Liabilities:

Last but not least, let's take a look at your liabilities—the debts and financial obligations you owe. This could include student loans, credit card debt, mortgages, or any other outstanding loans. Understanding your liabilities will help us gauge your debt load and develop strategies for paying off debt and improving your financial health.

Setting Realistic Goals:

Now that we have a clear understanding of your financial landscape, it's time to set some realistic goals for financial growth. Whether it's paying off debt, saving for a down payment on a house, or investing for retirement, setting SMART goals will give us a roadmap for success.

By understanding your current financial situation, you've laid the groundwork for future financial success. Keep tracking your progress, stay focused on your goals, and remember that every step you take brings you closer to financial independence.

Chapter 3.2: Budgeting Basics Made Easy

Mastering Your Money: Budgeting Basics Demystified

Welcome back, Money Queens, to Chapter 3 of "Money Queens," where we're demystifying budgeting and equipping you with practical tools and expert insights to take control of your financial destiny. Today, I'll guide you through the essential steps of budgeting, providing actionable tips and strategies to help you build a solid financial foundation and pave the way for long-term success. Let's dive in and empower ourselves with the knowledge and skills to master our money!

Understanding Budgeting Basics:

Budgeting is not just about numbers; it's about empowering yourself to make informed financial decisions that align with your goals and values. At its core, budgeting is a roadmap that guides your spending, savings, and investment decisions, ensuring that every dollar you earn is working towards your financial well-being. By gaining clarity on your income, expenses, and financial goals, you can make intentional choices that set you up for success.

Creating Your Monthly Budget:

The first step in mastering budgeting is creating a monthly budget tailored to your unique financial situation and goals. Start by listing all sources of income, including your salary, side hustle earnings, and any other money coming in. Next, identify your fixed expenses, such as rent or mortgage payments, utilities, groceries, and debt repayments. Don't forget to account for variable expenses like dining out, entertainment, and discretionary spending.

To streamline this process, consider using budgeting tools and apps like Mint, YNAB (You Need a Budget), or Personal Capital, which can automatically categorize your expenses and track your spending in real-time. These tools provide valuable insights into your spending habits and help you stay on track with your budgeting goals.

Tracking Your Expenses:

Once you've created your budget, the next step is to track your expenses throughout the month. Keep a close eye on your spending, recording every purchase and categorizing it according to your budget categories. This allows you to identify areas where you may be overspending and make adjustments as needed.

One effective strategy for tracking expenses is the envelope method, where you allocate cash into designated envelopes for different spending categories, such as groceries, dining out, and entertainment. When the cash in an envelope runs out, you know it's time to stop spending in that category for the month. This hands-on approach can help you stay disciplined and avoid overspending.

Adjusting Your Spending Habits:

As you track your expenses, you may uncover patterns or trends that reveal opportunities for improvement. Maybe you're spending more than you realized on non-essential items, or perhaps you're paying for subscriptions or memberships that no longer serve you. Take a critical look at your spending habits and identify areas where you can cut back or reallocate resources towards your financial goals.

Empowering Yourself with Practical Tips:

Throughout this section, I'll be sharing practical tips and expert insights to help you make the most of your budgeting efforts. Consider implementing strategies like the 50/30/20 rule, where 50% of your income goes towards needs, 30% towards wants, and 20% towards savings and debt repayment. Additionally, automate your savings contributions and bill payments to ensure consistency and avoid missed payments.

By mastering budgeting fundamentals and implementing practical strategies, you've taken a significant step towards financial empowerment and long-term success. Keep tracking your expenses, adjusting your spending habits, and prioritizing your financial goals. With a solid budget in place, you have the power to take control of your finances and create the life of your dreams.

Chapter 3.3: The Power of Emergency Funds: Your Financial Safety Net

Building Resilience: Harnessing the Strength of Emergency Funds

Welcome back, Money Queens, to Chapter 3 of "Money Queens," where we're delving into one of the most critical components of financial security: the emergency fund. Today, I'll illuminate the significance of having an emergency fund, provide you with actionable strategies to kick-start your savings, and equip you with valuable tools and resources to fortify your financial resilience. Let's embark on this journey to secure your future with confidence and grace.

Understanding the Essence of Emergency Funds:

An emergency fund isn't just a savings account—it's your lifeline during times of financial uncertainty. Picture it as your personal safety net, ready to catch you when unexpected expenses or financial setbacks arise. Whether it's a medical emergency, sudden job loss, or major home repair, having a robust emergency fund in place ensures that you can weather the storm without resorting to high-interest debt or depleting your long-term savings. It's the cornerstone of financial stability and peace of mind.

Setting Concrete Savings Goals:

To build an effective emergency fund, you need to establish clear savings goals tailored to your unique circumstances. Start by assessing your monthly expenses and determining how much you'd need to cover three to six months' worth of living expenses. This includes essentials like rent or mortgage payments, utilities, groceries, insurance premiums, and transportation costs. By having a specific target in mind, you can create a roadmap for your savings journey and stay motivated to reach your goals.

Automating Contributions for Consistency:

Consistency is key when it comes to building an emergency fund. Automating your savings contributions is a powerful way to ensure that you're consistently setting aside money for emergencies. Set up automatic transfers from your checking account to your designated emergency fund account each time you receive your paycheck. Treat these contributions as non-negotiable commitments to your financial well-being, just like you would with your other monthly expenses.

Exploring Strategies to Boost Savings:

While automating contributions is a great start, there are additional strategies you can employ to accelerate your emergency fund savings. Consider conducting a thorough audit of your expenses to identify areas where you can cut back and redirect those funds towards your emergency fund. Look for opportunities to increase your income through side hustles, freelance gigs, or selling unused items. Every extra dollar you save brings you closer to your savings goals.

Valuable Tools and Resources:

To streamline your savings efforts and stay on track with your emergency fund goals, consider leveraging budgeting apps and tools like Mint, YNAB (You Need a Budget), or Personal Capital. These platforms can help you track your expenses, set savings goals, and monitor your progress in real-time. Additionally, websites like Bankrate or NerdWallet offer valuable insights and resources on building emergency funds and managing personal finances.

By understanding the essence of emergency funds and implementing proactive savings strategies, you're taking decisive steps to fortify your financial resilience. Keep setting concrete savings goals, automating contributions for consistency, and exploring creative ways to boost your savings. With a robust emergency fund as your financial safety net and valuable tools at your disposal, you'll be well-equipped to navigate life's uncertainties and emerge stronger than ever. Keep shining, queens!

Chapter 4.1: Decoding Investments: From Stocks to Real Estate

Navigating the Investment Landscape: A Beginner's Guide to Building Wealth

Welcome, Money Queens, to Chapter 4 of "Money Queens," where we're demystifying the world of investments and empowering you to build wealth for the future. Today, I'll simplify complex investment concepts, introduce you to various investment options, and provide you with practical tips and resources to kick-start your investment journey. Let's dive in and equip you with the knowledge and confidence to make informed investment decisions.

Understanding Different Investment Options:

Investing may seem like venturing into uncharted waters, but with the right knowledge, you can navigate the investment landscape with confidence. Let's explore some of the most common investment options:

1. **Stocks:** Stocks represent ownership in a company, and when you invest in stocks, you're essentially buying a share of that company's profits and losses. Stocks offer the potential for high returns over the long term, but they also come with higher risks due to market volatility.
2. **Bonds:** Bonds are debt securities issued by governments or corporations to raise capital. When you invest in bonds, you're essentially lending money to the issuer in exchange for

periodic interest payments and the return of your principal investment at maturity. Bonds are generally considered safer than stocks but offer lower returns.
3. **Mutual Funds:** Mutual funds pool money from multiple investors to invest in a diversified portfolio of stocks, bonds, or other assets. By investing in mutual funds, you gain access to a professionally managed portfolio without the need for individual stock or bond selection. Mutual funds offer diversification and are suitable for investors seeking a hands-off approach to investing.
4. **Real Estate:** Real estate investing involves purchasing properties with the aim of generating rental income or capital appreciation. Real estate can be a lucrative investment option, offering steady cash flow and potential tax benefits. However, it requires significant capital and ongoing maintenance.

Choosing the Right Investment Account:

Once you understand the different types of investments, the next step is to choose the right investment account to hold your investments. Common investment accounts include individual brokerage accounts, retirement accounts like IRAs (Individual Retirement Accounts) or 401(k)s, and education savings accounts like 529 plans.

When selecting an investment account, consider factors such as tax implications, investment options, fees, and withdrawal restrictions. For long-term goals like retirement, retirement accounts offer tax advantages and should be prioritized. For shorter-term goals, individual brokerage accounts provide flexibility but may be subject to capital gains taxes.

Setting Investment Goals:

Before diving into investing, it's essential to define your investment goals and time horizon. Are you investing for retirement, a down payment on a home, or your child's education? Your investment goals will dictate your investment strategy, risk tolerance, and asset allocation.

For long-term goals like retirement, you can afford to take more significant risks and invest primarily in stocks for higher growth potential. For short-term goals, such as buying a house in the next few years, you'll want to prioritize capital preservation and invest in less volatile assets like bonds or cash equivalents.

By demystifying complex investment concepts and providing practical guidance, you're well-equipped to take the first steps towards building wealth through investment. Keep exploring investment options, choosing the right investment account, and setting clear investment goals aligned with your financial aspirations. With knowledge, patience, and a long-term perspective, you'll navigate the investment landscape with confidence and achieve financial success. Keep shining, queens!

Chapter 4.2: Exploring Alternative Investments: Real Estate, Cryptocurrency, and Beyond

Diversifying Your Portfolio: Unlocking the Potential of Alternative Investments

Welcome back, Money Queens, to Chapter 4 of "Money Queens," where we're broadening your investment horizons and delving into alternative investment opportunities that go beyond traditional stocks and bonds. Today, I'll introduce you to real estate investment, cryptocurrency, and other alternative assets, providing you with insights, strategies, and practical advice to diversify your investment portfolio and unlock new avenues for wealth accumulation. Let's embark on this journey to explore the exciting world of alternative investments and take your financial journey to new heights.

Exploring Alternative Investment Opportunities:

While stocks and bonds are fundamental components of any investment portfolio, alternative investments offer unique opportunities for diversification and potentially higher returns. Let's take a closer look at some popular alternative investment options:

1. **Real Estate Investment:** Investing in real estate involves purchasing properties with the aim of generating rental income or capital appreciation. Real estate offers tangible assets that can provide steady cash flow, potential tax benefits, and protection against inflation. However, it requires significant capital investment, ongoing maintenance, and careful due diligence.
2. **Cryptocurrency:** Cryptocurrency, such as Bitcoin and Ethereum, has gained popularity as a digital or virtual form of currency. Cryptocurrency investments offer the potential for high returns but come with significant volatility and regulatory uncertainty. Investors should conduct thorough research, understand the technology behind cryptocurrencies, and carefully assess their risk tolerance before investing in this asset class.
3. **Alternative Assets:** Beyond real estate and cryptocurrency, alternative investments encompass a wide range of assets, including commodities, precious metals, art, collectibles, and peer-to-peer lending platforms. Alternative assets provide diversification benefits and can hedge against market volatility, but they may also be illiquid and difficult to value.

Evaluating Alternative Investment Options:

Before diving into alternative investments, it's essential to conduct thorough research and due diligence to evaluate their potential risks and rewards. Consider factors such as historical performance, market trends, regulatory environment, and liquidity constraints. Consult with financial advisors or investment professionals to assess the suitability of alternative investments for your portfolio and financial goals.

Diversifying Investment Portfolios:

Diversification is the key to building a resilient investment portfolio that can weather market fluctuations and achieve long-term growth. By incorporating alternative investments into your portfolio alongside traditional assets like stocks and bonds, you can spread risk and capture opportunities across different asset classes and market cycles. Remember to rebalance your portfolio periodically to maintain your desired asset allocation and risk profile.

By expanding your investment horizons and considering alternative assets, you're diversifying your portfolio and unlocking new opportunities for wealth accumulation. Keep exploring alternative investment options, conducting thorough research, and consulting with financial professionals to make informed investment decisions. With a well-diversified portfolio and a strategic approach to investing, you'll be well-positioned to achieve your financial goals and secure your financial future.

Chapter 4.3: Diversification: The Key to Building a Resilient Investment Portfolio

Strengthening Your Financial Fortress: Mastering the Art of Diversification

Welcome, Money Queens, to Chapter 4 of "Money Queens," where we're diving into one of the fundamental principles of investing: diversification. Today, I'll emphasize the importance of building a resilient investment portfolio that can withstand market fluctuations by incorporating diversification strategies. I'll explain the concept of diversification, provide practical strategies for implementation, and empower you to create well-balanced investment portfolios tailored to your financial goals and risk tolerance. Let's fortify your financial fortress and pave the way for long-term success.

Understanding the Power of Diversification:

Diversification is the strategy of spreading your investments across different asset classes, industries, and geographic regions to reduce risk and enhance returns. By diversifying your portfolio, you can mitigate the impact of volatility in any single investment and capture opportunities across various market segments. Diversification is the cornerstone of building a resilient investment portfolio that can weather market downturns and achieve consistent growth over time.

Practical Strategies for Diversification:

1. **Asset Allocation:** Start by determining your asset allocation—the mix of stocks, bonds, and other asset classes in your portfolio. Consider your investment goals, time horizon, and risk tolerance when establishing your asset allocation. A diversified portfolio typically includes a combination of stocks for growth, bonds for income, and alternative assets for added diversification.
2. **Geographic Diversification:** Expand your investment horizons beyond domestic markets by diversifying across geographic regions. Investing in international stocks and emerging markets can provide exposure to different economies, currencies, and growth opportunities. Consider allocating a portion of your portfolio to global funds or exchange-traded funds (ETFs) for geographic diversification.
3. **Sector Diversification:** Avoid concentration risk by diversifying across different sectors and industries. Industries like technology, healthcare, consumer staples, and financials may perform differently under varying market conditions. By spreading your investments across multiple sectors, you can reduce the impact of sector-specific downturns on your portfolio.

Illustrating the Benefits of Diversification:

Through real-life examples and case studies, let's illustrate the benefits of diversification in action. Imagine two investors—one who concentrates all their investments in a single stock or sector and another who diversifies their portfolio across various asset classes and industries. During a market downturn or industry-specific downturn, the diversified investor is better positioned to minimize losses and preserve wealth compared to the concentrated investor.

By mastering the art of diversification and implementing practical strategies in your investment portfolio, you're strengthening your financial fortress and paving the way for long-term success. Keep diversifying across asset classes, industries, and geographic regions to mitigate risk and capture opportunities for growth. With a well-balanced and diversified portfolio, you'll navigate market fluctuations with confidence and achieve your financial goals.

Chapter 5.1: Retirement Planning for Millennials

Securing Your Golden Years: A Comprehensive Guide to Retirement Planning

Welcome, Money Queens, to Chapter 5 of "Money Queens," where we're diving into the critical topic of retirement planning for millennial women. Today, I'll emphasize the importance of early retirement planning, regardless of your age, and provide you with actionable strategies to secure your financial future in retirement. From understanding the unique challenges millennials face to practical tips for getting started, let's embark on this journey to ensure your golden years are truly golden.

Why Retirement Planning Matters, Even in Your 20s:

Many millennials underestimate the importance of retirement planning, assuming they have plenty of time to save for retirement. However, starting early is key to building a substantial nest egg and achieving financial security in retirement. Here's why retirement planning matters, even in your twenties:

1. **Longer Life Expectancies:** Millennials are expected to live longer than previous generations, which means they'll need more savings to support themselves throughout retirement. Starting early allows you to take advantage of compound interest and maximize the growth potential of your investments over time.
2. **Uncertainty of Social Security:** With the future of Social Security uncertain, millennials can't rely solely on government benefits to fund their retirement. By proactively saving and investing for retirement, you can create a reliable source of income independent of Social Security.

3. **Rising Cost of Living:** The cost of living continues to rise, making it essential to build a retirement nest egg that can keep pace with inflation. Starting early allows you to gradually increase your savings contributions over time and stay ahead of inflation.

Practical Tips for Getting Started:

1. **Set Clear Retirement Goals:** Start by defining your retirement goals and envisioning the lifestyle you want to enjoy in retirement. Consider factors such as where you want to live, how you want to spend your time, and any anticipated expenses, such as travel or healthcare.
2. **Calculate Your Retirement Needs:** Estimate how much you'll need to fund your desired lifestyle in retirement. Use online retirement calculators or consult with a financial advisor to determine your retirement savings target based on factors like your current age, desired retirement age, life expectancy, and expected expenses.
3. **Maximize Retirement Savings Vehicles:** Take advantage of retirement savings vehicles like employer-sponsored retirement plans (e.g., 401(k), 403(b)) and individual retirement accounts (IRAs). Contribute enough to your employer's retirement plan to qualify for any matching contributions, and consider maxing out your contributions to tax-advantaged accounts.
4. **Invest Wisely for the Long Term:** Allocate your retirement savings across a diversified portfolio of investments based on your risk tolerance and time horizon. Consider a mix of stocks, bonds, and other asset classes to balance growth potential with risk mitigation. Regularly review and rebalance your portfolio as needed to stay on track with your retirement goals.

By recognizing the importance of early retirement planning and implementing practical strategies to secure your financial future, you're taking proactive steps towards achieving financial security and independence in retirement. Keep setting clear retirement goals, maximizing retirement savings vehicles, and investing wisely for the long term. With dedication, discipline, and a long-term perspective, you'll build a robust retirement nest egg that allows you to enjoy the fruits of your labor in your golden years.

Chapter 5.2: Navigating Employer-Sponsored Retirement Accounts: 401(k), 403(b), and IRA

Unlocking the Power of Employer-Sponsored Retirement Accounts: Your Roadmap to Retirement Savings

Welcome back, Money Queens, to Chapter 5 of "Money Queens," where we're navigating the complex landscape of employer-sponsored retirement accounts. Today, I'll guide you through the ins and outs of 401(k), 403(b), and Individual Retirement Accounts (IRA), empowering you to maximize their benefits and achieve long-term financial security. From understanding how these accounts work to practical tips for optimizing contributions, let's embark on this journey to unlock the power of retirement savings.

Understanding Employer-Sponsored Retirement Accounts:

Employer-sponsored retirement accounts, such as 401(k) and 403(b) plans, are valuable tools for saving for retirement. These accounts allow you to contribute a portion of your pre-tax income to a retirement savings plan, where it can grow tax-deferred until retirement. Additionally, many employers offer matching contributions, effectively doubling your savings.

Individual Retirement Accounts (IRA) offer similar tax advantages but are not tied to employment. Traditional IRAs allow you to contribute pre-tax dollars, while Roth IRAs accept after-tax contributions and offer tax-free withdrawals in retirement.

Maximizing Retirement Account Benefits:

1. **Choose the Right Retirement Account:** Consider factors such as employer offerings, investment options, fees, and

contribution limits when choosing a retirement account. If your employer offers a 401(k) or 403(b) plan with matching contributions, prioritize contributions to maximize the employer match.

2. **Navigate Investment Options:** Once you've enrolled in a retirement plan, it's essential to choose the right investments for your portfolio. Most retirement plans offer a variety of investment options, including mutual funds, index funds, and target-date funds. Consider your risk tolerance, time horizon, and investment goals when selecting investments.
3. **Optimize Contributions:** Aim to contribute the maximum allowed to your employer-sponsored retirement account each year to take full advantage of tax-deferred growth and employer matching contributions. If you're unable to max out your contributions, contribute at least enough to qualify for any employer match, as it's essentially free money.
4. **Consider IRA Contributions:** In addition to employer-sponsored retirement accounts, consider contributing to an Individual Retirement Account (IRA) to supplement your retirement savings. Traditional IRAs offer tax-deferred growth, while Roth IRAs provide tax-free withdrawals in retirement. Maximize contributions to both accounts if possible, to diversify your tax exposure in retirement.

By understanding how these accounts work, maximizing their benefits, and optimizing contributions, you're taking proactive steps towards building a secure financial future in retirement. Keep prioritizing retirement savings, exploring investment options, and seeking guidance from financial professionals as needed. With diligence and determination, you'll unlock the full potential of your retirement accounts and achieve your long-term financial goals.

Chapter 5.3: The Magic of Compound Interest: Starting Early for a Wealthy Retirement

Unleashing the Power of Compound Interest: Your Key to a Wealthy Retirement

Welcome back, Money Queens, to Chapter 5 of "Money Queens," where we're uncovering the secrets of compound interest and its transformative impact on building wealth for retirement. Today, I'll unveil the magic of compound interest, explain how it works, and show you why starting to save for retirement early is the ultimate key to financial abundance in your golden years. Through practical examples and illustrations, let's harness the power of compound interest and set you on the path to a wealthy retirement.

Understanding Compound Interest:

Compound interest is often referred to as the eighth wonder of the world, and for a good reason. Unlike simple interest, which is calculated solely on the initial principal amount, compound interest takes into account both the initial principal and the accumulated interest over time. As a result, your savings grow exponentially over time, leading to substantial wealth accumulation.

The Power of Starting Early:

The most significant advantage of compound interest is its reliance on time. The earlier you start saving for retirement, the more time your money has to grow and compound. Let's illustrate this with a practical example:

Suppose two individuals, Sarah and Lisa, each start saving for retirement at different ages. Sarah begins saving $500 per month at age 25 and continues until age 65, while Lisa starts saving the same amount at age 35 and continues until age 65. Despite saving for the same number of years and contributing the same amount, Sarah ends up with a significantly larger retirement nest egg due to the extra years of compounding.

Practical Strategies for Maximizing Compound Interest:

1. **Start Early:** The key to maximizing compound interest is to start saving for retirement as early as possible. Even small contributions made in your twenties can grow into substantial sums over time, thanks to the power of compounding.

2. **Consistent Contributions:** Make regular contributions to your retirement savings accounts to ensure consistent growth over time. Set up automatic transfers or payroll deductions to make saving effortless and habitual.
3. **Reinvest Dividends and Interest:** Reinvest any dividends or interest earned on your investments to compound your returns further. Over time, reinvested dividends can significantly boost the growth of your investment portfolio.
4. **Avoid Early Withdrawals:** Resist the temptation to withdraw funds from your retirement accounts prematurely, as this can disrupt the power of compound interest. Instead, let your savings continue to grow and compound undisturbed until retirement.

Congratulations, Money Queens, you've completed the section on the magic of compound interest in Chapter 5 of "Money Queens"! By understanding the power of compounding, starting early, and making consistent contributions to your retirement savings, you're laying the foundation for a wealthy and financially secure future. Keep harnessing the magic of compound interest, prioritizing retirement savings, and staying committed to your long-term financial goals. With time on your side and the power of compounding at your disposal, you'll achieve financial abundance in retirement and live the life of your dreams.

Chapter 6.1: Building Wealth at Any Age

The Roadmap to Financial Independence: Tailored Investing Strategies for Every Life Stage

Welcome, Money Queens, to Chapter 6 of "Money Queens," where we're charting the course to financial independence with tailored investment strategies for every stage of life. Today, I'll guide you through investing strategies designed to align with your individual financial goals, risk tolerance, and life circumstances. From your twenties to retirement age and beyond, let's explore asset allocation, portfolio diversification, and investment vehicle selection to build wealth steadily throughout your life.

Investing Strategies for Every Stage of Life:

1. **Investing in Your 20s:**
   - **Start Early:** Take advantage of compounding by starting to invest in your twenties. Even small contributions can grow into significant sums over time.
   - **Embrace Growth:** Focus on growth-oriented investments, such as stocks and equity mutual funds, to capitalize on long-term growth potential.
   - **Take Risks:** In your twenties, you have time on your side to recover from market downturns. Don't be afraid to take calculated risks and invest in higher-risk, higher-reward assets.
2. **Investing in Your 30s:**
   - **Balance Growth and Stability:** As you enter your thirties, consider shifting towards a more balanced investment approach. Allocate a portion of your portfolio to more stable assets like bonds and diversify across asset classes.
   - **Save for Multiple Goals:** In addition to retirement, start saving for other financial goals, such as buying a home, starting a family, or pursuing further education.
3. **Investing in Your 40s:**
   - **Focus on Preservation:** As you approach your forties, prioritize capital preservation and risk management. Review your asset allocation and adjust it to reflect your changing risk tolerance and financial goals.
   - **Maximize Retirement Contributions:** Take advantage of catch-up contributions to retirement accounts if you haven't already done so. Maximize contributions to employer-sponsored plans and consider additional contributions to IRAs.
4. **Investing Beyond Retirement:**

- **Generate Passive Income:** In retirement, focus on generating passive income streams to supplement your retirement savings. Consider investments in dividend-paying stocks, real estate investment trusts (REITs), and annuities.
- **Stay Engaged:** Even in retirement, stay actively involved in managing your investments. Regularly review your portfolio, rebalance as needed, and stay informed about market trends and economic developments.

By tailoring your investment strategies to your life stage, financial goals, and risk tolerance, you're laying the foundation for long-term financial success and independence. Keep investing consistently, diversifying your portfolio, and staying informed about investment opportunities. With dedication and discipline, you'll build wealth steadily throughout your life and achieve the financial freedom you deserve.

Chapter 6.2: Overcoming Common Financial Challenges: Debt, Student Loans, and More

Conquering Financial Hurdles: Practical Solutions for Debt, Student Loans, and Beyond

Welcome back, Money Queens, to Chapter 6 of "Money Queens," where we're tackling common financial challenges head-on. Today, I'll address the prevalent issues of debt, student loans, and other financial obligations faced by millennial women. I'll provide you with practical strategies for managing and reducing debt, navigating student loan repayment options, and overcoming financial setbacks with resilience and determination. Let's empower you to conquer financial hurdles and regain control of your financial future.

Understanding Common Financial Challenges:

1. **Debt:** Many millennial women struggle with various forms of debt, including credit card debt, personal loans, and medical bills. High-interest debt can quickly spiral out of control if left unchecked, making it essential to address debt promptly and strategically.
2. **Student Loans:** Student loan debt is a significant burden for many millennial women, hindering their financial progress and delaying important milestones like homeownership and retirement savings. Navigating the complexities of student loan repayment options can be overwhelming but essential for managing debt effectively.

Practical Solutions for Overcoming Financial Challenges:

1. **Budgeting:** Start by creating a realistic budget that accounts for your income, expenses, and debt obligations. Identify areas where you can cut expenses and reallocate funds towards debt repayment.
2. **Debt Consolidation:** Consider consolidating high-interest debt into a single, lower-interest loan to simplify repayment and reduce overall interest costs. Explore options such as balance transfer credit cards, personal loans, or home equity loans.
3. **Student Loan Repayment:** Investigate repayment options for student loans, such as income-driven repayment plans, loan consolidation, or loan forgiveness programs. Choose the option that best aligns with your financial situation and long-term goals.
4. **Emergency Fund:** Build an emergency fund to cover unexpected expenses and avoid relying on high-interest debt in times of financial need. Aim to save three to six months' worth of living expenses in a readily accessible savings account.
5. **Seek Professional Help:** If you're struggling to manage debt or navigate student loan repayment options, don't hesitate to seek help from financial professionals, credit counselors, or student loan advisors. They can provide personalized guidance and support tailored to your unique circumstances.

By implementing practical solutions and strategies for managing debt, navigating student loans, and building financial resilience, you're taking proactive steps towards achieving financial freedom. Keep budgeting effectively, exploring debt consolidation options, and seeking professional guidance as needed. With determination and perseverance, you'll overcome financial obstacles and emerge stronger on the path to financial independence.

Chapter 6.3: Turning Financial Goals into Actionable Plans: Dream Big, Achieve Bigger

From Dreams to Reality: Crafting Your Path to Financial Success

Welcome back, Money Queens, to the final section of Chapter 6 in "Money Queens," where we're transforming your financial goals into actionable plans for success. Today, I'll guide you through the process of setting specific, measurable, achievable, relevant, and time-bound (SMART) goals and provide you with practical strategies for creating a financial action plan that propels you towards your dreams. Let's dive in and turn your aspirations into reality.

Setting SMART Financial Goals:

1. **Specific:** Define your financial goals with clarity and specificity. Instead of vague aspirations like "saving money" or "paying off debt," set specific targets such as "saving $10,000 for a down payment on a home" or "paying off $5,000 in credit card debt within one year."
2. **Measurable:** Make your goals measurable by quantifying them in terms of dollars, percentages, or specific milestones. This allows you to track your progress over time and stay motivated as you work towards achieving your objectives.
3. **Achievable:** Set goals that are realistic and attainable based on your current financial situation, resources, and timeline. While it's essential to dream big, ensure that your goals are

within reach and feasible with diligent effort and commitment.
4. **Relevant:** Align your financial goals with your values, priorities, and long-term aspirations. Consider how each goal contributes to your overall financial well-being and personal fulfillment, ensuring that they resonate with your values and objectives.
5. **Time-bound:** Establish clear deadlines or target dates for achieving each goal to create a sense of urgency and accountability. Setting time-bound goals helps you stay focused, motivated, and disciplined in pursuing your objectives.

Crafting Your Financial Action Plan:

1. **Reflect on Your Values:** Begin by reflecting on your values, priorities, and long-term aspirations. Consider what matters most to you and how your financial goals align with your values and life vision.
2. **Identify Financial Objectives:** Break down your overarching financial goals into smaller, actionable objectives that you can tackle incrementally. Prioritize your objectives based on their importance and urgency, focusing on those that will have the most significant impact on your financial well-being.
3. **Develop Strategies and Tactics:** Once you've identified your financial objectives, develop strategies and tactics for achieving each goal. Consider what steps you need to take, resources you'll need, and potential obstacles you may encounter along the way.
4. **Create a Timeline:** Establish a timeline or action plan outlining specific tasks, deadlines, and milestones for each goal. Break down your goals into manageable chunks and assign deadlines to keep yourself on track and accountable.
5. **Monitor and Adjust:** Regularly monitor your progress towards your financial goals and adjust your action plan as needed. Stay flexible and adaptable in response to changing circumstances or unexpected challenges, and celebrate your successes along the way.

Resources and Tools for Success:

1. **Budgeting Apps:** Use budgeting apps like Mint, YNAB (You Need a Budget), or Personal Capital to track your spending, set savings goals, and monitor your progress towards financial objectives.
2. **Financial Planning Software:** Consider using financial planning software like Quicken or Tiller Money to create detailed financial plans, analyze your spending habits, and forecast your financial future.
3. **Online Courses and Workshops:** Take advantage of online courses, workshops, and webinars offered by financial experts and organizations to enhance your financial literacy, develop money management skills, and learn about investing, budgeting, and retirement planning.
4. **Books and Publications:** Explore books, articles, and publications on personal finance, investing, and wealth-building to expand your knowledge and gain insights from experts in the field.

By setting SMART goals, crafting a financial action plan, and leveraging resources and tools for success, you're well-equipped to achieve your financial aspirations and build a future of abundance and fulfillment. Keep dreaming big, taking decisive action, and staying committed to your financial goals. With determination, resilience, and the right strategies in place, you'll turn your dreams into reality and create the life of your dreams.

Chapter 7.1: Protecting Your Financial Future

Safeguarding Your Tomorrow: Mastering Insurance Basics for Financial Security

Welcome, Money Queens, to Chapter 7 of "Money Queens," where we're diving into the essential topic of insurance and its pivotal role in securing your financial future. Today, I'll unravel the fundamentals of insurance—health, life, and disability—and empower you to make informed decisions to protect yourself and your loved ones from financial risks. Let's delve into insurance basics and equip you with the knowledge and tools you need to safeguard your tomorrow.

Understanding Insurance Basics:

1. **Health Insurance:** Health insurance is your first line of defense against unexpected medical expenses and healthcare costs. It provides coverage for doctor visits, hospital stays, prescription medications, and preventive care services. Understanding the key components of health insurance, such as premiums, deductibles, copayments, and coinsurance, is crucial for choosing the right coverage that meets your needs and budget.
2. **Life Insurance:** Life insurance plays a vital role in providing financial security for your loved ones in the event of your death. It provides a death benefit to your beneficiaries, helping them cover living expenses, mortgage payments, education costs, and other financial obligations. Consider factors such as your age, health, income, and family situation when determining the type and amount of life insurance coverage you need.
3. **Disability Insurance:** Disability insurance is a crucial safeguard against income loss due to disability or illness that prevents you from working. It provides a source of replacement income to cover living expenses, medical bills, and other financial obligations if you become unable to work due to a disabling injury or illness. Understanding the different types of disability insurance—short-term and long-term—and their coverage limits, waiting periods, and benefit periods is essential for ensuring adequate protection.

Mastering Insurance Basics:

1. **Assess Your Insurance Needs:** Start by assessing your insurance needs based on your financial situation, lifestyle, and family responsibilities. Consider factors such as your health, income, assets, debts, and dependents when

determining the type and amount of insurance coverage you require.
2. **Research Your Options:** Research different insurance providers, policies, and coverage options to find the best fit for your needs and budget. Compare premiums, deductibles, coverage limits, and policy features to ensure you're getting the most value for your money. Employers or having certain memberships can have perk programs, be sure to check your options!
3. **Consult with Experts:** Consider seeking guidance from insurance agents, financial advisors, or insurance brokers who can help you navigate the complexities of insurance and tailor coverage to your specific needs. They can provide personalized advice, answer your questions, and help you make informed decisions.
4. **Review and Update Regularly:** Regularly review your insurance coverage to ensure it remains adequate and up-to-date with your evolving financial situation and life circumstances. Update your policies as needed to reflect changes such as marriage, childbirth, home purchase, or career advancements.

By mastering the fundamentals of health insurance, life insurance, and disability insurance, you're taking proactive steps to protect yourself and your family from financial risks. Keep assessing your insurance needs, researching your options, and consulting with experts to ensure you have the right coverage in place. With the right insurance protection, you'll have peace of mind knowing that you're safeguarding your financial future and your loved ones' well-being.

Chapter 7.2: Estate Planning Made Simple: Wills, Trusts, and Power of Attorney

Securing Your Legacy: A Comprehensive Guide to Estate Planning Essentials

Welcome back, Money Queens, to Chapter 7 of "Money Queens," where we're demystifying estate planning and empowering you to secure your legacy for future generations. Today, I'll walk you through the essential components of estate planning—wills, trusts, powers of attorney, and savvy strategies like the 1031 exchange—and provide you with practical advice for creating a comprehensive estate plan that ensures your assets are distributed according to your wishes. Let's simplify estate planning concepts and equip you with the knowledge and tools you need to protect your estate and legacy.

Understanding Estate Planning Essentials:

1. **Wills:** A will is a critical document in estate planning that outlines your wishes for the distribution of your assets after your death. It allows you to specify beneficiaries, designate guardians for minor children, and appoint an executor to oversee the administration of your estate. Your will can also outline instructions for the use of a 1031 exchange to defer capital gains tax if your estate includes property holdings.
2. **Trusts:** Trusts are powerful tools for estate planning that offer benefits such as asset protection, probate avoidance, and privacy. Consider establishing trusts such as revocable living trusts or irrevocable trusts to hold your assets and ensure they are managed and distributed according to your wishes. By placing your property into a trust, such as a Qualified Personal Residence Trust (QPRT) or a Grantor Retained Annuity Trust (GRAT), you can minimize estate taxes and provide ongoing support for your loved ones. Additionally, having LLCs tied to trusts can provide an extra layer of protection for your assets.
3. **Powers of Attorney:** A power of attorney is essential for estate planning as it grants authority to another person to make financial or healthcare decisions on your behalf in case of incapacity. Appointing a trusted individual to act as your agent ensures that your affairs are managed and decisions are made according to your wishes.

Creating a Comprehensive Estate Plan:

1. **Assess Your Estate:** Evaluate your assets, liabilities, and personal circumstances to determine your estate planning needs. Consider factors such as the value and nature of your assets, potential tax implications, and the needs of your beneficiaries.
2. **Consult with Professionals:** Seek guidance from estate planning attorneys, financial advisors, or estate planning professionals who can help you develop a tailored plan to meet your goals. They can provide personalized advice, draft legal documents, and ensure compliance with relevant laws and regulations.
3. **Draft Legal Documents:** Work with professionals to draft essential estate planning documents, including wills, trusts, powers of attorney, and advance healthcare directives. Ensure these documents accurately reflect your wishes and intentions and are legally valid and enforceable.
4. **Review and Update Regularly:** Regularly review and update your estate plan to account for changes in your financial situation, family dynamics, or legal regulations. Updating your plan ensures that it remains relevant and effective in achieving your goals.

By understanding the importance of wills, trusts, powers of attorney, and strategic planning techniques like the 1031 exchange and LLC incorporation, you're taking proactive steps to protect your estate and legacy. Keep assessing your estate planning needs, consulting with professionals, and updating your plan regularly to ensure it remains current and effective. With a well-crafted estate plan in place, you'll have peace of mind knowing that your wishes will be honored, and your loved ones will be provided for.

Chapter 7.3: Safeguarding Your Wealth: Strategies to Protect Against Financial Risks

Fortifying Your Financial Fortress: Proven Strategies for Wealth Protection

Welcome back, Money Queens, to the final section of Chapter 7 in "Money Queens," where we're delving into additional strategies to safeguard your wealth and shield it from financial risks. Today, we'll explore the crucial aspects of asset protection, cybersecurity, and risk management, providing you with actionable steps to fortify your financial fortress and achieve greater peace of mind in your financial journey.

Asset Protection Strategies:

1. **Liability Insurance:** Liability insurance is a fundamental component of asset protection, providing coverage in the event of lawsuits or claims against you. Consider securing adequate liability coverage through homeowners, renters, auto, and umbrella insurance policies to shield your assets from potential legal liabilities.
2. **Umbrella Policies:** Umbrella insurance policies offer an extra layer of liability protection beyond the limits of standard insurance policies. They provide additional coverage for legal expenses, damages, and settlements in case of lawsuits or liability claims that exceed the limits of your primary insurance policies.
3. **Legal Entities:** Establishing legal entities such as limited liability companies (LLCs) and trusts can provide valuable asset protection benefits. LLCs offer liability protection for business owners and real estate investors by separating personal and business assets and shielding them from potential lawsuits or creditor claims. Trusts, such as irrevocable trusts or spendthrift trusts, can protect assets from creditors and ensure their intended use for beneficiaries.

Cybersecurity Measures:

1. **Protecting Personal Information:** Safeguard your personal and financial information from online threats by implementing cybersecurity best practices. Use strong, unique passwords for online accounts, enable multi-factor authentication, and regularly update security software and systems to prevent unauthorized access to your data.

2. **Securing Financial Transactions:** Exercise caution when conducting financial transactions online and avoid sharing sensitive information on unsecured websites or public Wi-Fi networks. Use secure, encrypted connections for online banking, shopping, and other financial activities to protect your financial information from cybercriminals.

Risk Management Strategies:

1. *Diversification:* Diversifying your investment portfolio across different asset classes, industries, and geographic regions can help mitigate investment risk and minimize potential losses during market downturns. Consider diversifying your investments through a mix of stocks, bonds, real estate, and alternative assets to spread risk and enhance portfolio resilience.
2. *Emergency Preparedness:* Prepare for unexpected financial emergencies by maintaining an adequate emergency fund to cover living expenses, medical bills, and other essential costs in case of job loss, illness, or other unforeseen circumstances. Aim to set aside three to six months' worth of living expenses in a liquid, easily accessible savings account to weather financial storms.

Congratulations, Money Queens, you've completed the section on safeguarding your wealth and protecting against financial risks in Chapter 7 of "Money Queens"! By implementing asset protection strategies, cybersecurity measures, and risk management techniques, you're fortifying your financial fortress and preserving your hard-earned wealth for the future. Keep prioritizing asset protection, stay vigilant against cyber threats, and maintain a proactive approach to risk management to achieve greater peace of mind and financial security.

Chapter 8.1: Navigating Financial Milestones with Grace

Unlocking the Door to Your Dream Home: A Millennial's Guide to Homeownership

Welcome to Chapter 8 of "Money Queens," where we're embarking on a journey to navigate one of life's most significant financial milestones with grace: buying your first home. Whether you're dreaming of a cozy bungalow, a chic urban loft, or a suburban sanctuary, I'm here to provide you with valuable insights and practical tips to guide you through the exciting journey of homeownership.

Buying Your First Home: Tips for Millennial Homebuyers

Congratulations, Money Queens, you're ready to take the plunge into homeownership! In this chapter, I'll share valuable insights and practical tips to help you navigate the process of buying your first home with confidence and ease. Let's dive in:

1. **Budgeting for a Down Payment:** Start by assessing your financial situation and setting a realistic budget for your down payment. Aim to save at least 20% of the home's purchase price to qualify for a conventional mortgage and avoid private mortgage insurance (PMI). Explore down payment assistance programs and explore alternative financing options if saving a large down payment seems daunting.
2. **Understanding Mortgage Options:** Familiarize yourself with the various mortgage options available to millennial homebuyers, including fixed-rate mortgages, adjustable-rate mortgages, FHA loans, and VA loans. Compare interest rates, terms, and fees from multiple lenders to find the best mortgage option that fits your financial needs and goals.
3. **Navigating the Homebuying Process:** Educate yourself about the homebuying process from start to finish, including pre-approval, house hunting, making an offer, and closing. Work with a reputable real estate agent who understands your needs and preferences and can guide you through each step of the process. Be prepared to act quickly in a

competitive market and negotiate effectively to secure the best deal on your dream home.
4. **Finding the Right Real Estate Agent:** Choose a real estate agent who specializes in working with millennial homebuyers and has a proven track record of success in your desired area. Look for an agent who listens to your needs, communicates effectively, and advocates for your best interests throughout the homebuying process.
5. **Evaluating Neighborhoods:** Research and explore different neighborhoods to find the perfect location for your new home. Consider factors such as proximity to work, school districts, amenities, safety, and future development plans. Visit neighborhoods at different times of the day and talk to residents to get a feel for the community's vibe and lifestyle.
6. **Negotiating Purchase Offers:** Work with your real estate agent to craft a competitive purchase offer that reflects the current market conditions and aligns with your budget and preferences. Be prepared to negotiate with sellers on price, contingencies, and closing costs to reach a mutually beneficial agreement. Stay flexible and open-minded throughout the negotiation process to increase your chances of success.

By following these valuable insights and practical tips, you're well-equipped to navigate the homebuying process with confidence and grace. Keep dreaming big and taking decisive action towards achieving your homeownership goals. Your dream home awaits!

Chapter 8.2: Planning for Marriage and Family: Combining Finances with Your Partner

Building a Financial Future Together: A Guide to Combining Finances as a Couple

Welcome to Chapter 8 of "Money Queens," where we're delving into the intricacies of planning for marriage and family, and the journey of combining finances with your partner. Whether you're newly engaged, preparing to tie the knot, or starting a family, I'm here to guide you through the process of merging your financial lives and laying the groundwork for a harmonious and prosperous future together.

Planning for Marriage and Family: Combining Finances with Your Partner

Congratulations, Money Queens, on taking the next step in your relationship journey! In this chapter, we'll explore the essential considerations and practical strategies for merging finances with your partner and planning for marriage and family. Let's dive in:

1. **Open Communication:** Start by having open and honest conversations with your partner about your financial values, goals, and concerns. Discuss your individual financial situations, including income, expenses, debts, and assets, and identify areas of alignment and potential differences. Establishing a foundation of trust and transparency is crucial for building a strong financial partnership.
2. **Shared Financial Goals:** Work together to define shared financial goals and priorities for your life together as a couple. Whether it's buying a home, saving for retirement, or starting a family, aligning your financial aspirations ensures that you're both working towards common objectives. Set SMART goals—specific, measurable, achievable, relevant, and time-bound—and create a roadmap to achieve them together.
3. **Merging Finances:** Decide on the best approach for merging your finances, whether it's combining all accounts, maintaining separate accounts, or adopting a hybrid approach. Consider factors such as income disparities, individual financial obligations, and personal preferences when determining how to structure your joint finances. Create a joint budget that reflects your shared income, expenses, and financial goals, and establish clear guidelines for managing money as a couple.
4. **Navigating Financial Decisions:** Make major financial decisions together as a team and involve each other in the

decision-making process. Whether it's buying a car, making home improvements, or investing in the stock market, consult with your partner and consider each other's input before proceeding. Practice active listening, compromise, and mutual respect to ensure that both partners feel valued and empowered in financial decisions.

5. **Financial Compatibility:** Assess your financial compatibility as a couple and address any differences or conflicts that may arise. Be open to compromise and find creative solutions to reconcile differences in financial habits, attitudes, and priorities. Consider seeking guidance from a financial advisor or couples counselor to navigate challenging conversations and develop a shared understanding of your financial values and goals.

6. **Prenuptial Agreements:** Discuss the role of prenuptial agreements in protecting individual assets and addressing financial concerns in the event of divorce or separation. While prenuptial agreements may not be romantic, they can provide clarity and peace of mind for both partners by outlining expectations for asset division, spousal support, and other financial matters. Consult with a family law attorney to understand the legal implications of prenuptial agreements and determine if one is appropriate for your situation.

By embracing open communication, shared financial goals, and mutual respect, you're laying the groundwork for a successful and harmonious financial future together. Keep working as a team, supporting each other's financial aspirations, and nurturing your relationship with love, trust, and financial harmony. Your journey towards building a prosperous life together starts now!

Chapter 8.3: Achieving Financial Independence: Your Ticket to Freedom and Fulfillment

Unleashing Your Financial Freedom: The Path to Achieving Independence and Fulfillment

Welcome back to the final section of Chapter 8 in "Money Queens." Here, we're delving deep into the transformative concept of financial independence—the cornerstone of a life lived on your own terms. In this section, we'll explore the multifaceted nature of financial independence, its profound impact on your quality of life, and actionable strategies for making it a reality. Get ready to rewrite your financial narrative and step into a future brimming with freedom and fulfillment.

Defining Financial Independence:

Let's start by painting a clear picture of what financial independence truly means. Beyond the numbers and spreadsheets, financial independence is a state of empowerment—a state where you have the freedom to make choices without being shackled by financial constraints. It's the ability to pursue your passions, explore new opportunities, and live life on your terms, without the burden of financial worries weighing you down. Financial independence is about designing a life that aligns with your values, aspirations, and dreams, and having the resources to turn those dreams into reality.

Exploring the Principles of FIRE:

One powerful movement that embodies the ethos of financial independence is FIRE (Financial Independence, Retire Early). At its core, FIRE is a lifestyle philosophy centered around achieving financial freedom at a young age, allowing individuals to retire early and pursue their passions. While FIRE may not be the ultimate goal for everyone, its principles—such as mindful spending, intentional saving, and strategic investing—can serve as a roadmap for anyone seeking financial independence. By adopting the mindset of FIRE, you can accelerate your journey towards financial freedom and unlock a world of possibilities for the future.

Practical Strategies for Financial Independence:

Now, let's dive into the actionable strategies that can propel you towards financial independence:

1. **Maximize Savings:** Start by evaluating your current spending habits and identifying areas where you can trim expenses. Automate your savings and set up separate accounts for different financial goals, such as emergency funds, retirement savings, and investment accounts. By prioritizing savings and living below your means, you can build a solid financial foundation and accelerate your path to independence.
2. **Invest Strategically:** Take a proactive approach to investing by diversifying your portfolio across various asset classes, including stocks, bonds, real estate, and alternative investments. Consider consulting with a financial advisor to develop a customized investment strategy that aligns with your risk tolerance and long-term goals. By harnessing the power of compounding returns and staying disciplined in your investment approach, you can build wealth steadily over time and achieve financial independence sooner.
3. **Increase Income Streams:** Explore opportunities to boost your income through side hustles, freelance work, or entrepreneurial ventures. Leverage your skills, talents, and passions to create multiple streams of income that can supplement your primary earnings and accelerate your journey towards financial independence. Whether it's starting a small business, monetizing a hobby, or freelancing in your spare time, diversifying your income sources can provide greater financial stability and flexibility.
4. **Reduce Expenses:** Adopt a minimalist mindset and question the true value of each purchase before making it. Look for ways to cut unnecessary expenses, negotiate better deals on recurring bills, and prioritize spending on experiences rather than material possessions. By embracing frugality and mindful spending, you can free up more resources for saving and investing, bringing you closer to your goal of financial independence.
5. **Embrace Financial Mindset:** Cultivate a mindset of abundance, gratitude, and empowerment that empowers you to take control of your financial destiny. Challenge limiting beliefs about money and success and visualize your desired financial future with clarity and conviction. By adopting a

positive and proactive mindset, you can overcome obstacles, stay focused on your goals, and navigate the ups and downs of your financial journey with confidence and resilience.

By embracing the principles of financial independence, envisioning a life of freedom and fulfillment, and taking proactive steps towards your goals, you're charting a course towards a brighter and more abundant future. Keep nurturing your financial independence journey, stay focused on your goals, and never lose sight of the limitless possibilities that await you on the path to financial freedom. Your journey towards financial independence starts now—embrace it with confidence, determination, and unwavering belief in your ability to create the life of your dreams.

Chapter 9.1: Cultivating Financial Confidence and Empowerment

Embracing Your Financial Victories: Building Confidence on the Road to Success

Welcome to Chapter 9 of "Money Queens," where we embark on a journey of celebration and empowerment as we explore the power of acknowledging and celebrating our financial wins. In this chapter, we'll dive into the importance of recognizing and honoring the progress we make on our financial journey, no matter how small. Get ready to embrace your victories, build confidence, and fuel your momentum towards financial success.

Celebrating Your Financial Wins: Small Victories Lead to Big Successes

Congratulations, Money Queens! You've made it this far on your financial journey, and it's time to pause, reflect, and celebrate the milestones you've achieved along the way. In this section, we'll explore the transformative power of celebrating your financial wins, no matter how modest they may seem.

Why Celebrate Financial Wins?

Before we dive into the how-to's of celebrating financial victories, let's first understand why it's essential to acknowledge and celebrate our progress. Celebrating financial wins serves multiple purposes:

1. **Motivation and Momentum:** Celebrating your achievements provides a much-needed boost of motivation and momentum to keep moving forward on your financial journey. Recognizing your progress reinforces positive behaviors and encourages you to continue making smart financial decisions.
2. **Gratitude and Appreciation:** By taking the time to celebrate your financial wins, you cultivate a sense of gratitude and appreciation for the efforts you've put into improving your financial situation. It allows you to acknowledge the hard work, discipline, and sacrifices that have contributed to your success.
3. **Confidence Building:** Celebrating your financial victories builds confidence and self-belief, empowering you to tackle bigger challenges and set loftier goals. Each win—no matter how small—serves as a reminder of your ability to overcome obstacles and achieve success in your financial life.

Strategies for Celebrating Financial Wins:

Now that we understand the importance of celebrating financial wins, let's explore some practical strategies for making the most of these moments:

1. **Reward Yourself:** Treat yourself to a well-deserved reward for reaching a financial milestone, whether it's a small indulgence like a fancy coffee or a bigger splurge like a weekend getaway. Choose rewards that align with your values and bring you joy without derailing your financial progress.
2. **Share Your Achievements:** Share your financial wins with friends, family, or members of your support network who will celebrate your success with you. Sharing your

achievements not only amplifies the joy of the moment but also reinforces your commitment to your financial goals.
3. **Reflect and Appreciate:** Take time to reflect on the journey that led to your financial win and appreciate the progress you've made. Journaling or meditation can be powerful tools for processing your emotions, expressing gratitude, and fostering a positive mindset.
4. **Set New Goals:** Use your financial victories as inspiration to set new, challenging goals that will propel you further on your journey towards financial success. Whether it's paying off another debt, increasing your savings rate, or investing in a new opportunity, let your wins fuel your ambition and drive.

Congratulations, Money Queens, you've completed Chapter 9 of "Money Queens"! By embracing the practice of celebrating your financial wins, you're not only acknowledging your progress but also building confidence, motivation, and momentum on your path to financial success. Keep celebrating every step forward, no matter how small, and remember that each victory brings you closer to the life of abundance and fulfillment you deserve. Here's to many more financial wins on your journey ahead!

Chapter 9.2: Embracing Financial Challenges: Turning Setbacks into Comebacks

Triumph Over Trials: Transforming Financial Challenges into Victories

Welcome to Chapter 9 of "Money Queens," where we confront the inevitable financial challenges that arise on our journey to financial independence. In this section, we'll explore how to reframe setbacks as opportunities for growth and resilience, equipping you with the tools and mindset needed to overcome obstacles and emerge stronger than ever.

Navigating Financial Challenges with Resilience:

Financial challenges are an unavoidable aspect of life, but how we respond to them can make all the difference. Instead of viewing setbacks as insurmountable roadblocks, we can choose to see them as opportunities for growth, learning, and transformation. In this section, we'll delve into practical strategies for navigating financial challenges with resilience and grace.

Reframing Setbacks as Opportunities:

The first step in overcoming financial challenges is to reframe them as opportunities for growth and empowerment. Rather than dwelling on the negative aspects of a setback, focus on the lessons it can teach you and the strengths it can help you develop. By adopting a growth mindset, you can approach challenges with optimism and resilience, knowing that every obstacle you overcome brings you one step closer to your goals.

Practical Strategies for Overcoming Obstacles:

Now, let's explore some practical strategies for overcoming financial challenges and bouncing back stronger than ever:

1. **Assess the Situation:** Take a step back and assess the nature and severity of the financial challenge you're facing. Identify the root causes of the setback and brainstorm potential solutions to address them effectively.
2. **Seek Support:** Don't be afraid to reach out for support from friends, family, or financial professionals who can offer guidance, encouragement, and practical assistance. Surround yourself with a supportive network of people who believe in your ability to overcome challenges and succeed.
3. **Stay Positive:** Maintain a positive outlook and focus on solutions rather than dwelling on the problem. Practice gratitude, self-care, and mindfulness to cultivate resilience and keep your spirits high during challenging times.
4. **Learn and Adapt:** View setbacks as opportunities for learning and growth, and use them as catalysts for personal and financial development. Identify lessons learned from the

experience and apply them to future situations to prevent similar setbacks from occurring.
5. **Take Action:** Once you've identified potential solutions, take decisive action to implement them and address the challenges head-on. Break down larger goals into smaller, manageable tasks, and celebrate each small victory along the way.

By embracing financial challenges as opportunities for growth and resilience, you're cultivating the strength, determination, and wisdom needed to overcome any obstacle that comes your way. Remember that setbacks are not failures but stepping stones on the path to success. Keep persevering, stay resilient, and trust in your ability to turn setbacks into comebacks. You've got this!

Chapter 9.3: Paying It Forward: Empowering Other Women on Their Financial Journeys

Building a Sisterhood of Financial Empowerment: Lifting Each Other Higher

Welcome to the final section of Chapter 9 in "Money Queens," where we delve into the transformative power of paying it forward and empowering other women on their financial journeys. In this segment, we'll explore the importance of community, collaboration, and advocacy in creating a more inclusive and equitable financial landscape for all.

The Power of Community and Collaboration:

As we've journeyed through the pages of "Money Queens," we've recognized the significance of community and collaboration in achieving financial goals. Now, it's time to harness that power and extend a helping hand to other women who are navigating their own financial journeys. By coming together in solidarity and support, we can amplify our collective impact and create lasting change.

Sharing Knowledge and Resources:

One of the most valuable gifts we can offer each other is the gift of knowledge and resources. Whether it's sharing personal finance tips, recommending useful tools and resources, or providing guidance based on our own experiences, every bit of information shared can make a difference in someone else's life. Let's commit to being generous with our knowledge and resources, knowing that by lifting others, we lift ourselves as well.

Mentorship and Guidance:

Mentorship plays a crucial role in empowering women to reach their full potential, especially in the realm of finance. Consider offering mentorship to other women who are earlier in their financial journeys, providing guidance, encouragement, and support as they navigate challenges and pursue their goals. Likewise, don't hesitate to seek out mentorship opportunities for yourself, learning from the wisdom and experiences of those who have walked the path before you.

Financial Education and Advocacy:

Advocating for financial education and gender equality in finance is another powerful way to pay it forward. Get involved in initiatives that promote financial literacy among women and advocate for policies that address gender disparities in the financial industry. By raising awareness and advocating for change, we can create a more inclusive and equitable financial future for all women.

By embracing the ethos of paying it forward and empowering other women on their financial journeys, you're not only making a positive impact on the lives of others but also contributing to the collective empowerment of women everywhere. Let's continue to lift each other higher, share our knowledge and resources, and advocate for a more inclusive and equitable financial landscape. Together, we can create a brighter and more prosperous future for all.

Chapter 10: Conclusion

Your Financial Reign Begins: Step into Your Power and Live Your Dreams

Welcome to the final chapter of "Money Queens," where we bring our journey to a close with renewed determination and empowered spirits. In this concluding segment, we'll reflect on the transformative insights gained throughout our exploration and set our sights on a future filled with financial abundance and fulfillment.

Seizing Your Financial Destiny:

As we bid farewell to the pages of "Money Queens," let's remember that financial empowerment is not just a distant dream but a tangible reality within our grasp. Armed with the knowledge, tools, and inspiration gleaned from our journey, we have the power to shape our financial destinies and create lives of abundance and fulfillment.

Setting Your Course for Success:

Now is the time to translate our newfound wisdom into action. Let's set concrete financial goals that reflect our aspirations and values, whether it's building wealth, achieving financial independence, or pursuing our passions without financial constraints. By committing to our goals with unwavering determination, we lay the foundation for a future filled with possibility and promise.

Embracing the Journey with Optimism:

Along the road to financial empowerment, we will encounter challenges, setbacks, and detours. But let's remember that every obstacle is an opportunity for growth and every setback is a stepping stone to success. With optimism and resilience as our guides, we navigate the twists and turns of the journey with grace and fortitude, knowing that our dreams await on the other side.

Stepping into Your Power:

As we bid adieu to "Money Queens," let's embrace our power as millennial women and take ownership of our financial destinies with unwavering confidence and purpose. Let's stand tall, speak boldly, and claim our rightful place as architects of our own financial futures. Together, we can shatter glass ceilings, defy expectations, and create a world where every woman reigns supreme in her financial life.

As you close this book and embark on the next chapter of your financial journey, remember that your fabulous financial future starts now. Take action, live your dreams, and never underestimate the power you hold within. With determination, resilience, and a dash of sparkle, you can achieve anything you set your mind to. Here's to a future filled with prosperity, abundance, and limitless possibility. Cheers to you, Money Queens!

Stay Inspired: Resources for Your Financial Journey

As we wrap up our journey through "Money Queens," I want to equip you with an array of resources tailored to support and inspire you on your ongoing financial path. Below, you'll find a curated selection of books, podcasts, websites, and online communities that specifically cater to female empowerment and financial literacy. Explore these resources to deepen your knowledge, find motivation, and connect with like-minded individuals who share your financial aspirations.

Books:

1. **"Smart Women Love Money: 5 Simple, Life-Changing Rules of Investing" by Alice Finn -** A guide designed specifically for women, offering practical advice and empowering strategies for taking control of your financial future through investing.
2. **"Financially Forward: How to Use Today's Digital Tools to Earn More, Save Better, and Spend Smarter" by Alexa Von Tobel -** Learn how to leverage technology to optimize your financial life, from budgeting and investing to managing debt and planning for the future.
3. **"Girl, Get Your Money Straight: A Sister's Guide to Healing Your Bank Account and Funding Your Dreams in 7 Simple Steps" by Glinda Bridgforth -** A comprehensive financial guide tailored to the unique challenges and opportunities faced by women, providing actionable steps to achieve financial wellness and abundance.

Podcasts:

1. **Clever Girls Know: The Podcast - Hosted by Bola Sokunbi,** this podcast empowers women to take control of their finances and build wealth through practical advice, expert interviews, and inspiring stories of financial success.
2. **Women & Money - Suze Orman,** one of America's most trusted personal finance experts, shares her insights and wisdom on money matters specifically tailored to women, covering topics such as investing, retirement, and financial independence.
3. **Brown Ambition - Join hosts Mandi Woodruff and Tiffany Aliche** for candid conversations about money,

career, and success, with a focus on empowering women of color to achieve their financial goals and dreams.

Websites:

1. **Ellevest (www.ellevest.com) -** A digital investing platform designed for women, offering personalized investment portfolios and financial planning tools tailored to women's unique financial needs and goals.
2. **Girls on the Money (www.girlsonthemoney.com) -** Founded by financial educator and stock market expert Mabel Nunez, this website offers online courses, workshops, and resources to help women become confident investors and master their finances.
3. **The Budgetnista (www.thebudgetnista.com) -** Created by financial educator Tiffany Aliche, The Budgetnista offers practical advice, tools, and resources to help women achieve financial freedom and live their best lives on a budget.

Online Communities:

1. **Women Who Money (www.womenwhomoney.com) -** Join this community of women-focused personal finance bloggers and experts for support, guidance, and inspiration on your financial journey.
2. **The Financial Gym (www.financialgym.com) -** Become a member of this online financial wellness community, where women come together to receive personalized financial coaching, support, and accountability to achieve their money goals.
3. **The Female Money Doctor Community -** Connect with Dr. Nikki Ramskill and other like-minded women in this supportive online community focused on financial education, empowerment, and transformation.

Remember, Money Queens, the resources and support you need to achieve financial success are at your fingertips. Dive into these valuable tools, connect with empowering communities, and continue your journey to financial independence with confidence and determination. Here's to your continued growth, abundance, and prosperity!

www.ingramcontent.com/pod-product-compliance
Lightning Source LLC
Chambersburg PA
CBHW030501220526
45464CB00006B/2599